SPEAK WITH THE SUN

To
B E

SPEAK WITH THE SUN

David Campbell

" At midnight speak with the Sun "

HENRY VAUGHAN

1949
CHATTO & WINDUS
LONDON

PUBLISHED BY

Chatto & Windus

LONDON

*

Clarke, Irwin & Company Ltd.

TORONTO

ACKNOWLEDGMENTS

I thank *The Bulletin* in which most of these poems first appeared; and Douglas Stewart for the use of maps and compass.

CONTENTS

HUMPING A BLUEY

" They may call me both daft and mad,"
Sang a swagie to his blue;
" They click their tongue at the life I've led,
But I care not for old nor young
For I sing with the magpie's tongue:"
And the coolibah tree said " True."

" They click their tongue or split their side,"
Sang a swagie to his blue,
" But I am steadfast in the pride
That of all mortals I am blest—
I dance with the lyre bird in her nest:"
And the coolibah tree said " True."

" They split their side but what care we? "
Sang a swagie to his blue.
" I lie on grass and you lie on me,
And sweet dew falls from the morning air
On rock and bush and in my hair:"
And the coolibah tree said " True."

" At sight of me young babies cry,"
Sang a swagie to his blue,
" With mouths as wide as the open sky;
But what care I when by this tree
The fox and the rabbit lie down with me:"
And the coolibah tree said " True."

7

" Oh, boys throw stones with a tutored aim,"
Sang a swagie to his blue,
" But though their learning may send me lame,
I know more of heaven and hell
Than fathers or schoolmasters tell:"
And the coolibah tree said " True."

" And young girls titter behind their hand,"
Sang a swagie to his blue.
" They sell their souls for a golden band;
And this is truth, upon my life—
I'd rather have you than the banker's wife:"
And the coolibah tree said " True."

" Though the banker has both wife and gold,"
Sang a swagie to his blue,
" And walls to keep out sun and cold,
He'll die alone; but when I'm done
Then you and I and the tree are one:"
And the coolibah tree said " True."

HARRY PEARCE

I sat beside the red stock route
And chewed a blade of bitter grass
And saw in mirage on the plain
A bullock wagon pass.
Old Harry Pearce was with his team.
" The flies are bad ", I said to him.

The leaders felt his whip. It did
Me good to hear old Harry swear,
And in the heat of noon it seemed
His bullocks walked on air.
Suspended in the amber sky
They hauled the wool to Gundagai.

He walked in Time across the plain,
An old man walking in the air,
For years he wandered in my brain;
And now he lodges here.
And he may drive his cattle still
When Time with us has had his will.

THE STOCKMAN

The sun was in the summer grass,
The coolibahs were twisted steel:
The stockman paused beneath their shade
And sat upon his heel,
And with the reins looped through his arm
He rolled tobacco in his palm.

His horse stood still. His cattle dog
Tongued in the shadow of the tree,
And for a moment on the plain
Time waited for the three.
And then the stockman licked his fag
And Time took up his solar swag.

I saw the stockman mount and ride
Across the mirage on the plain;
And still that timeless moment brought
Fresh ripples to my brain:
It seemed in that distorting air
I saw his grandson sitting there.

THE SUNDOWNER'S DREAM

He sat by the fire;
It burned with a black flame
In the fluid air
And he told me his dream.

" There was no one but I.
The yellow hills stood
Against the coloured sky
As I walked down the road.

" I boiled my billycan
By an eye-clear spring
Where the town road ran;
And I heard the billy sing:

" ' To the right,' it sang
So I turned to the right,
And the billy rang
Like a bell that night.

" By dawn I had come
To a sunstruck plain
Where magpie was dumb
For the want of rain;

" Yet on the distant ground
I saw a great sea flow
Before me, and I found
The billy was a crow."

The black fire burned,
And a tune came from
The billy as I turned
Back the way I had come.

KOOKABURRA

Ants in the red earth,
Red ants in red stone
Between the cold sky and the cracked plain.
Alone
A dry tree lifts withered arms and prays for
     rain.
What is this mirth
Splitting the earth, the air;
Iron-hard in the hot brain,
Deriding prayer?
It is the Jack again.
Though the snake writhes in the dust of noon
It will not die
Till black night brings the white moon.

THE TRAPPER'S SONG

" In the bracken country,"
The trapper said to me,
" I am abroad before the sun;
The only man to see
The first light to liquefy the leaves
On every standing tree.

" From the early sunlight
The magpie takes her note.
Her voice is heard, then like the bird
I loosen up my throat;
And she and I sing to the day
A song we have by rote."

" It is an idle lyric:"
The trapper cocked an eye;
" One singing from a bracken brake,
The other from the sky,
That bird and beast are at their spring
And may give death the lie.

" I gather up my rabbits
And down the bracken lane
I sing a song that life is young
And scorn the mortal strain
Of rabbits nodding at my belt
That say my song is vain."

OLD TOM DANCES

The grass is bleached like a barmaid's hair,
As soft as her arms in the evening air,
And old Tom dances in the failing light,
A foot in day and a foot in night.

Old Tom dances; he skips like a hare;
And the rising moon had better beware
For Tom and his pockets are stuffed with rum
And he dares the moon and 'em all to come.

" Whoa there, bullocks! " he tells his feet;
" There's rum in the billy, there's rum for meat.
Up there, Baldy! Up there, Roan! "
And he talks to his feet in a bullocky's tone.

Who is that peeping through sunset eyes
As the sun sinks and the stars rise?
He thought that boy forty years dead
For he pulled the blankets over his head.

The boy looks out, his kelpie fears
Forgotten, forgotten the twisted years
And the fiend who stares from the dam's still
        glass;
And he lies in locks of moonlit grass.

SUMMER

When hatters talk to ears of grain
And hawks cut figures in the sky
And squatters, while they search for rain,
Wipe their back paddocks from their eye;
When 'hopper swarms are sleek and fat
And Welcome's eaten from the mat:
Oh, country wives leave country men
And barmaid Nell's their sweetheart then.

When heat-swamps on the dusty plain
Recede to mock the travelling sheep
And weather-prophets' words are vain
And crows delight while cockies weep;
When kelpies tongue though Clancy calls,
And loungers shoulder hotel walls:
Oh, tramps and fat commercial men
Call barmaid Nell their sweetheart then.

WINTER

When magpies sing in sky and tree
And colts like dragons snuff the air
And frosts paint hollows white till three
And lamp-lit children skip their prayer;
Then Meg and Joan at midnight lie
And quake to hear the dingoes cry
Who nightly round the white church stone
Snap at their tails and the frosty moon.

When stockmen lapped in oilskin go
And lambing ewes on hill-tops bleat
And crows are out and rain winds blow
And kettles simmer at the grate;
Then Meg and Joan at midnight lie
And quake to hear the dingoes cry
Who nightly round the white church stone
Snap at their tails and the weeping moon.

WINTER STOCK ROUTE

Here where red dust rose
To raddle sheep and men
And the kelpie tongued at noon,
Silence has come again.
The great-boled gumtrees bow
Beneath their load of snow.

The drover and his dray
Have gone; and on this hill
I find myself alone
And Time standing still.
Printless the white road lies
Before my quiet skis.

But where my skis trace
Their transient snow furrow,
For generations both
Man and beast will follow.
Now in this winter passage
I cross the deserted stage.

SPRING HARES

There is a stranger on the stock route.
See his red beard and eyes of flame!
The sky's his swag; the magpies shout
Across a continent his name:
It is the sun! It is the dawn!—
Bless the day that I was born.

There are two boxers through the gumtrees;
Their shadows spar on the far hill,
Counter and close. What giants are these?
Surprised, a pair of hares stand still.
It's a fine thing at your front gate
To see such angry lovers mate.

Bill is out on the red stallion;
His piebald mob crops blades of fire.
Trees burn, leaves melt; in conflagration
The big buck hare has his desire
Where the red ridge meets the spring sky,
Locked in the sun's irradiant eye.

SMALL-TOWN GLADYS

There are rows of bottles against the glass;
I look between and my hair's blonde grass,
My lips are berries and my skin is cream
And I fill my frock to the very brim
And twirl a curl when the sportsmen pass—
And I'm a good girl, I am.

They call me Glad and say I'm a queen.
I look in the glass and my eyes are green
And they talk to men though they make no sound
For it's love that makes the world go round;
But go too far and I say " Go on;
I am a good girl, I am."

In every novel I'm Lady Jane,
I use the book as a wicked fan,
And I sit on a stool and my fingers knit
A web to snare a sportsman's wit;
And they look at me as they look for rain,
But I'm a good girl, I am.

Under the willows, under the night,
Where schoolboys spy and the parson might,
I am the moon that rules the tides
Of men. And I shake and hold my sides
And I say " My make-up's an awful sight—
And I'm a good girl, I am."

" RACE BOOK, RACE BOOK, RACE BOOK FOR RANDWICK!"

Place your bet in the paddock with the flushed
    bookmaker,
That marsupial man who cups fat fist to call
The odds and lays the field for any taker;
Come, down your beer; come to the favourite's
    stall.

The chestnut stallion stands there like a king,
Pride in his carriage, eagles in his eye,
His mane the wind. Sun smooths his colouring
With gentle hand, falls flat on passers-by.

The groom stands in the shade. Twin horses
    ride
The pupils of his eyes. This stable boy
Scorns the lean tipster with a borrowed pride,
His whisper " Is the red the real McCoy? "

He is holding his joy in hand with a tight rein
Until the field turns into the straight for home
And the crowd stands up. He fondles his horse
    in pain
As once he fondled him on the tracks of Rome.

AT THE SHEEP-DOG TRIALS

What ancestors unite
Here in this red and white
Kelpie to define
His symmetry of line,

As crouched in burning dust
He halts both Time and beast?
The wethers stamp the ground,
At his will turn around.

He is of collie stock:
Austerity of rock
Has lent his mind and bone
The toughness of its stone.

And though for Border flocks
The collie and the fox
Fought tooth to tooth, they joined
And have the kelpie coined

Whose ears acutely set
Across the centuries yet
Hear the concordant sound
Of coupled horn and hound;

And as the moon the tides
The hidden vixen guides
With craft the blood that strains
And surges in his veins.

Those who stand and stare
At cripples in the fair
Have not the eyes to see
His blood's dignity

Where old adversaries meet,
As now on velvet feet
He moves to his master's call,
In action classical.

IN A SHAFT OF SUNLIGHT

In the sunlight among the rocks
Mica gleams and the thin red fox
Snaps and snarls and shows his teeth,
Stands erect with a hunter's faith;
And the magpies stall and dive.
Bird must build and fox must live.

Ah, but see death! Ripple of ice
In sunlight. Where dead timber lies
Beneath the overhanging bough
The black snake is moving now.
His passing makes no noise.
Look! Look now! Death's striking poise!

A river of wind flows through the trees,
Down the spine to shake the knees;
Shakes the gumnuts to the earth
To give the future forests birth
Where magpie, fox and snake
May hunt and die and men may quake.

LET EACH RIPEN

Where the horse and horseman go
Iron is clamorous on stone,
Spark and heavenly bluebell grow.
World enough for flesh and bone.
The black mare in the blue pool
Stamps her image and is still.

Where the tree would spread her bough
Cloud masses fill the chart;
There the skilled explorer now
Satisfies and steels the heart.
The aircraft sings in the thinning air,
Climbs the still momentous stair.

Let the living horseman ride:
Sweet and sensuous is earth's breath;
Scorned by the pilot in his pride,
It will open at his death.
Before his final bed is made
Let each ripen in his trade.

HATTER IN UTOPIA

" They have my curse," the hatter cried,
" Who got a thought with child,
Who wrote an answer in the sky
And tamed the brilliant wild
Scrub horses in the hill country
And the broad plain lands defiled."

" I was man and I was bird,"
I heard the hatter sing;
" I rode the immaculate cold air
Upon the eagle's wing.
Now bird looks down on ant and men
Walking in a ring."

" I was man and I knew pain."
Loud was the hatter's cry.
" I knotted a fist like a drought-parched tree
And shook it at the sky,
Yet found more truth in a pint of beer
Than your philosophy."

" I was man and I was fiend,"
The hatter said. " Ah well,
I knifed my mother for half-a-crown
And her blood flowed from the till.
Now priest and jurors share my curse
For they cheated me out of hell."

" Fiend or angel, saint or beast,"
I heard the hatter say—
" My love and I beneath the briar
Naked and sinning lay,
Yet the briar-rose on the briar tree
Shone like the milky way."

THE POSSUM AND THE MOON

I

Where a twisted tree
Split the rough sandstone,
I stood at night and heard
A possum scold the moon.

I listened for the cock
Who would call my dead
Grandfather from his grave
To my grandmother's bed.

I waited for the magpie
An hour before the dawn
To sing " Tan tara, boys! "
On old John Bax's horn.

I lifted up my hand
And made my ear a cup;
The skewbald dingo slept
At Brigalow Gap.

The only sounds I heard
That hour before the light
Were the tide in the leaves,
The possum's cry to the night.

II

I heard the possum cry
Beneath the yellow moon.
I said '' That moon was made
. From this same sandstone.''

The moon looked through the trees
And where her shadows stood,
Blackmen sprang upright;
They filled the ancient wood.

A tide ran through the leaves;
Otherwise a still
Hush lay on the bush
Where the shadows fell.

Like a lubra the land
Lay quiet, indifferent.
The shadows stole to the trees
At the moon's ascent.

CONROY'S GAP

The lorry climbs towards Conroy's Gap;
The driver and the moon are full,
For while he drank at The Shadow of Death
The moon lay down on his load of wool
And with a bale-hook in her hair
Like a willing girl she is sleeping there.

—He heard the trooper at the door,
He heard the barmaid catch her breath
And when the Swagman leapt the rails
He heard the rider laugh at death
Who rode as mountain horsemen ride
With Darby Munro at his side.—

The lorry moves past walls of stone;
The driver yawns and rubs his eyes:
A convict in a tailored suit
Is picking shale on the iron rise
And singing in the bitter cold
" I dig for truth in chains of gold."

The possum's eyes return the glare
Of headlights; dingoes hunt the hills
And pick the moonlight from dry bones
That once stood up in Burke and Wills.
As bristles stand on the dingo's hide—
The bones knit up; Burke thumbs a ride.

28

" Both beer and girls I loved," he said
" And yet my mind would not be still
Despite the inadequacy of flesh
To execute the spirit's will
In city or on desolate plain.
Wills, up man! T me to strive again."

The lightning strides across the ridge;
Wills strides between the falling steel;
A tommy-gun is in his hand
And men in green are at his heel,
While those beneath the Flemish grass
Cry " You'll be sorry," as they pass.

The lorry crosses Conroy's Gap.
Feel for the butt behind your ear;
Here are the matches, strike and cup
Your lean face in the red flare
And blink the mirage from your brain
Where Harry walks on moonshine.

THE KIDNEY AND THE WREN

A MELODRAMA

The jackass laughs in the white light;
The silence of the noon
Is shattered. From a crooked tree
He cackles like a loon.
The crow throws on his villainous cloak
In the footlights of the sun.

And though the lark, the thrush, the wren,
May hiss from stalls of briar,
The black crow looks from lidded eyes,
His voice is colder than the skies,
He pecks a young lamb's kidney out
And throws it to the choir.

And lo! The smallest little wren
Quits hissing, quits the thicket;
Sun glints from avaricious eye;
Her beak is quick to pick it.
A golden hawk drops from the sun;
The wren and lamb are one.

The jackass laughed in the white light;
The silence of the noon was shattered.
I asked him what the moral was?
He said " As if it mattered! "
He laughed aloud: " It was kid-stakes;
My favourite heroines are snakes."

BIRD CAGE

I

Those yellow spots on his sleek coat
A cause of great contentment are
To that fat thrush. And who can say
He is more vain than cooling star;
Or—this is his own comparison—
Less than great Napoleon?

The magpie singing his delight
An unskilled artisan may be;
In dinner suit of black and white
He only gets the sun for fee;
Yet sweetly still his notes will come
When all our instruments are dumb.

II

The hawk on convoy duty swings
Above the lanes of ewes and he,
When ground-lark from her cover springs,
Is beautiful in cruelty;
He makes the stockman catch his breath
Who is less intimate with death.

Regard that crow. His lambing cry
Has turned to skeletons the trees;
A universe is in his eye
And there the setting Pleiades;
Yet with a sharper appetite
He watches through the winter night.

III

For miles around the golden cock
Who takes his music from the sun,
Cries to the men whom once he woke
That they might pull their trousers on;
But though all night he sing his song
He cannot make an old man young.

The magpie then begins. He warms
The day with his familiar note,
And young men leap from lovers' arms
To see the ruffle of his throat
Who sings from twig so small you'd swear
That yogi-like he sat on air.

IV

On the grey blue bough
Of the blue grey tree
The magpie now
Works alchemy.

Where the crow of night
Was sitting, there
He in black and white
Is minting air.

No snake charmer's note
Such attention won;
With minute throat
He rules the sun:

From the bough at dawn
He sings, and high
The sun reborn
Lifts in the sky.

v

The cock intreats
In copper tone:
Lovers, spare conceits;
Kiss and be done.
His hen has laid
The morning sun.

Sparrows contend
In penny quartet:
Lovers, kiss and end;
Before you met
Their song was heard
By Juliet.

Lovers, away!
The magpies mould
Mintage of day;
Their looted gold
They steal from you
To make you cold.

33

c

Cackle eternity
And let that mad proud cock
Your spouse in this hen house
Hop, strut, till the hills rock,
Crow till he wake the sea.

Forgive that addled dawn
When on your star-scratched nest
You the egg earth gave birth;
This day reprieves the rest—
To-day a first child was born.

MORSE AT MIDNIGHT

Waking in your midnight bed
Hear the morse-key cricket sing
Above the footfalls of the clock;
Pull the blanket round your head:
Wrapt in sleep the morning cock
Has his crest beneath his wing.

Every living thing it seems
Sleeps. In bed and nest and lair
All are trafficking in dreams.
From their private worlds to this
Those at sea and in the air
Send their lonely messages

Troubling the winter night
With a whispered urgency.
So the wife who lies alone
Hears six hours before the light
Storm in air and storm at sea
Echoed in the cricket's drone.

Constant to her ancient track
Through the navigable stars
Soon the spinning earth will turn
House and city on her back
Around until another dawn
Filters through our window bars.

May the music of the key
Guide the tired pilot home
To the beacon's smaller light
Though the migratory storm,
That intruder enemy,
Prowls beneath the stars to-night.

May no lunar forces lift
To the moonlight on the deep
Swell of the Pacific, men
Who with whales and fishes sleep
Cradled in the current's drift
Whom the key shall call in vain.

SOLDIER'S SONG

Though I march until I drop
And my bed is sand,
I have filled the desert's cup
Harvested its land;
And this I learned from the desert wind,
From the sphinx it blows:
The Murray's source is in the mind
And at a word it flows.

Though I climb the bitter rock,
Jungle for a bed,
I can muster such a flock
As never Falkiner bred;
And this I learned from the tropic wind
Where the giant storm grows:
The Murray's source is in the mind
And at a word it flows.

THE SOLDIER AND THE MERMAID

This is as true as it is strange:
Tall grass is goose down;—
I walked over the bitter range,
Over the range and half way back
And carried an ocean in my pack:
In the green jungle.

It is an ocean I can hold;
Tall grass is goose down;—
Its tongue is sweet though its throat is
whorled
And locked in the shell's intricacies
Are all the sounds of the seven seas:
In the green jungle.

It is so small a sea its sand
Tall grass is goose down;—
Lies in the hollow of my hand;
Yet at my ear it sings and lo!
I hear the songs the great whales know:
In the green jungle.

Oh let it sigh into my ear:
Tall grass is goose down;—
The mermaids sing as they comb their hair
And coconut and fecus tree
Curl steep tops to break on me:
In the green jungle.

Oh mermaids comb their hair and sing;
Tall grass is goose down;—
I have bought one a golden ring
And I know all the sirens tell
As I sink beneath a midsea swell:
In the green jungle.

MEN IN GREEN

Oh, there were fifteen men in green,
Each with a tommy-gun,
Who leapt into my plane at dawn;
We rose to meet the sun.

We set our course towards the east
And climbed into the day
Till the ribbed jungle underneath
Like a giant fossil lay.

We climbed towards the distant range
Where two white paws of cloud
Clutched at the shoulders of the pass;
The green men laughed aloud.

They did not fear the ape-like cloud
That climbed the mountain crest
And hung from twisted ropes of air
With thunder in their breast.

They did not fear the summer's sun
In whose hot centre lie
A hundred hissing cannon shells
For the unwatchful eye.

And when on Dobadura's field
We landed, each man raised
His thumb towards the open sky;
But to their right I gazed.

For fifteen men in jungle green
Rose from the kunai grass
And came towards the plane.   My men
In silence watched them pass;
It seemed they looked upon themselves
In Time's prophetic glass.

Oh, there were some leaned on a stick
And some on stretchers lay,
But few walked on their own two feet
In the early green of day.

They had not feared the ape-like cloud
That climbed the mountain crest;
They had not feared the summer's sun
With bullets for their breast.

Their eyes were bright, their looks were dull,
Their skin had turned to clay.
Nature had met them in the night
And stalked them in the day.

And I think still of men in green
On the Soputa track
With fifteen spitting tommy-guns
To keep a jungle back.

WEATHER SYNOPSES

I

Storm made no declaration. Without warning, wind
Strode through defenceless borders, armed with bright
    hail
Sharper than the sun's sword. Look; Oh look
    behind!
From stormtroop cloud crow-paratroopers sail
Knife-beaked for slaughter. Torn is the steep hill-
    side,
Torn the ewe, the plotting heart and hand;
And wind is here to rip the tatter wide
For joy and fear alike are contraband.
Blow wind; beat hail; strike, you black veterans,
    home;
Lash, knock and probe! so long as the intricate
    heart
Still feels the pitch and terror of the storm.
There's something to be said for the weather's
    smart
And a world puffed up against you, for the rocking
    tree;
And there is a gust of joy in tragedy.

A steep ascent, mist like an undertow
Lapping and curling through the depth-charge trees
And a dream hand at the ankle, backs in the view
Where the conjuring eye for frost-woolled boulders
    sees
A fallen lamb and ewe. Oh the crow sings
And his song is desolation. Here there's no guide,
No warmth, no human comfort; only dark wings
And a sun like a cold young planet in the void.
Then see! The air's in blossom, like love, like fire;
And it is angel-tongued. At the last stride
Are morning, summit, magpies in a gyre,
Young lambs new-butting at their mothers' side,
Each rock and stone a fortune. And though mists
    return,
There is this region where they glow and burn.

III

So great a calm on earth and in the air!
The land's in doldrums; like a sunning cat
She licks herself with oceans. Smoke climbs his stair
And trees are loafers battening on the state;
They will not stir. Oh where is foreman Time?
Can he sit fishing now the job's half done,
Leaving us here for ever where no clock will chime
Though plan and bricks are ready? It's not to be borne.
Come, Time, about your business. Men, up and dress;
We'll set the man example. But though we buy
And sell and love and labour, hurry to press
And keep accounts, a cypher's in the sky;
And the cat-sea laves the extended land.
Soft! Do you feel? I felt a soft clawed hand.

THE TALLY

" What is it your fingers tell
When you stop to cross the street?
What I have I would not have
As he knows who loves me well;
The only kisses that I crave
Glorify my will's defeat,"
Said Joan and walked on.

" What is it your fingers tell
When the grey rain is falling down?
Light the light and press the bell,
Step into a velvet gown;
Sitting here before the glass
I defy the years that pass,"
Said Jean in spring green.

" What is it your fingers tell
When the factory whistles sound?
I have got a dress as well,
Sewn, hemmed and made to fit;
I will wear it with an air
Till I have a foot of ground
And no use for it."

COUNTRY BOARDING HOUSE

You'd do well to arrive here in daylight. Spinster pines
Complain continuously, sigh their set lines,
Knitting white socks of cloud or patching sunlight.
But oh! how malign they are, how they weep at night
Drawn up around the moonshine, warming stiff bones,
As if the old spent house had coals for stones.

" Do you remember the master? Blood in keen eyes
And age mere fancy-dress, a thin disguise
To be thrown off at midnight. He'd strike the
    board
And hang his wife and children on his word."
And the pines simper and gossip, sigh and tell over
His tales of drought and flood as did their lost lover.

The wind turns south, the pines shiver. They
    mourn
For a thin tired lady who walked upon the lawn
And held a flower cupped a moment. And the slant
    light
Blossomed for her and the flowers became more
    bright
And the sprinkled dust breathed out. She turned away
From Time who paused to pass the time of day.

"There was George," the pines sigh; " George,
    his mother's darling,
Climbing for cones, for the blue eggs of the
    starling,
Off on his pony, home by train from school
With a flask in his bag and a baby for that fool
Tow-headed housemaid. And—just think, my
    dear!—
He married the hussy later, or so I hear."

" And whom did John marry? " " I believe he
    married well,
Biscuits or steel. Yet he was forced to sell
When his curt father, angered by prying death,
Clouded his mirrored face with his last breath.
And now John's dead. He left a tolerant wife
And fifty a year to his sister for her life."

Pines weep, pines nod together, whisper and sway,
Murmur " To-morrow soon is yesterday."
Each year the sister comes, bones in black satin,
Pain and memory thinning while her bags fatten
With relics, locks of hair. At lunch and tea
She mourns like a dry sea-shell for its lost sea.

And each year trippers bring in the spring. The wattle
Remembers to be gay. Underground the battle
Of roots for sap; above, laughter and games,
Croquet, riding, tennis and christian names.
The old house yawns with doors and blinks with blinds
And flappers bounce in the saddle on pinched behinds.

But at night the pines take over. How they complain!
" Their manners, my dear! " New thoughts in his
    old brain,
The house troubles the sleepers. Laughter dies.
The magpie's promises are young men's lies,
Yet put your mouth here, hold me while the pines
    sigh
For this is Time's no-man's-land in which we lie.

FIGHTER PILOT'S MATE

Look! See the tiger! It lay asleep twenty years
Or played with toys and school books; but leapt awake
In a glistening sky, ready. And mauled by wild fears,
He twirled the horizon about his thumb and finger
As a schoolboy spins his cap. He was quick to steady,
To learn the mastery of eye and muscle,
The right button pressure. And in a high ice haze
He hunted with his eyes and guns ablaze.

Go ask the jungle. Whom should the tiger marry?—
A gentle girl, corn-fair, web-haired and merry.
Her love was sunlight; swift about her face
Starling emotions fluttered. There was the grace
Of sun with rain. And while she walked or shopped,
She'd sing above tight pain; but song and heart stopped,
Each time the post-boy passed her in a hurry.

Well, the war's underground. And who can blame
    him—
Cat whiskers shorn, delight locked up in hangar—
If he scorns saucer milk, seeks life, adventure
In pub and foreign arms? Would you have her tame
    him?

D

Now look again. Prize: find the missing girl.
At sundown I have seen a vivid eye,
Heard the branch break, the pad and feline snarl
Of beasts in their kitchen. But let her mother sigh,
On elephants of grief scorn love and hate
And scream for separation. She comes too late.
The tigress knows that she has found her mate.
The starlings have settled.
                           Still, if you wish to weep—
For sentimental endings are in fashion—
Weep for young Tommy warm in his baby carriage,
All licked and polished and reaching for the light;
Weep for the child conceived last Saturday night
Between the claw and reconciliation.

GREEK BOY AND GIRL WITH RIFLES

Against the vivid drop of sky
See where this sullen couple stand,
The tiger lashed within his eye,
The orchard crushed within her hand.

Here on this dusty road in Greece
The snipers' summer-lightning gleams
And each man greets his brother's face
Each time he slides the bolt and aims
Or wounds the one for whom he burns,
The darling of his mind and lust;
And voices plead within the loins
And cry a warning from the dust.

Oh you who stand above the plain
And wear a clouded human face
Are counters in a dead man's brain
Or guardians of a foreign peace;
But stand as you have ever stood,
Aggressor and victim of all wars;
And evening glistens with your blood
And streams are turbulent with your tears.

THE STORM

The tree is rooted deep. It stands stock still
And lets the storm brew witchcraft on the hill:
The granite air is golden. And now see,
Oh catch the breath at the small fierce dragonfly
Among the lightning. Taller than standing tree,
Butting the toppling stonework of cleft sky,
An aircraft sparks across immensity.

And the pilot, swallowed, yawns. You may be sure
His is the smile adjusted at the door
Where heart raps the summons. Did Jonah in the
    whale
Call up his pride and set astride his feet,
Still doubt's still voices, plotting the route he'd sail?
He feels the rudder quiver, sits to meet
The panel's doubtful screening of the gale.

And he is in the bonfire. Set a candle there
And cup it from the melting lips of air,
The kiss and rape of forces. O pilot sit well,
Flirting has set you in the witch's side
And you must act physician, save that still
White moth-flame from immensity of shade
Where gropes the witless tree upon the hill.

THE FORKING TREE

I said to my love, " Come with me
Where like lightning stands the tree."
But my love drew back in fright:
" There is a savage under it;
See his naked back and thigh,
See the mica in his eye
And the gesture of his arm—
And my father's house is warm."

I took her hand. " Come," I said,
" Though the leaves glow white and red."
But a convict sat in chains
Suffering the world's pains
Underneath the forking tree,
Hate and wonder in his eye:
" Look," he said, " beyond the rise
Wrapt in glory, China lies."

I said to my love, " Come," again.
The sun struck on the bitter plain
Where the lonely swagman stood,
And his murmur chilled the blood:
I have walked the twisted track,
Rods of sunlight on my back,
And I walked so far alone
That my brain returned to stone.

I took her pretty hand.   She came
Where the fire cured her shame
And the naked man was hushed
For he brought us all we wished
Peddling a hundred wares
From the misty hemispheres;
And our minds shook off the spell
Of the swagman's lonely tale.

THE SEASON OF THE YEAR

I

Set the bird within the tree,
Light the candles on the brier,
Sow a crop of oaten green,
Satisfy the eye and ear.
There is nothing left to do:
This is the season of the year.

There is nothing you need say.
When the bee is in the pear
And the wind comes silently,
Turn and find your image there
In the iris of her eye:
This is the season of the year.

Ask no foolish question. Let
Figured sunlight smooth her hair,
Warm the kindly earth and sky:
There is nothing she need wear
When the oats are girdle-high:
This is the season of the year.

Then sigh, then grieve,
Whisper in an oaten ear,
Bid the bird and bud good-day:
They have said it all before
Who in grave and suburb lie:
This is the season of the year.

II

The hare leaps in the bright green
    morning,
Pirouettes in rainbow light
While within the changing tree
Setting air to melody
For the fantastic shadow's clowning
Sits the bird of day and night.

See the happy couples come
Now the magic light is falling.
Those who listen to the tune
Are mysteriously one
Moving to the dancer's time
While the hidden bird is calling.

III

My love is good and kind,
She is a sweetie;
Go through the world, you'll find
No one so preety.
She has lips to kiss
And she most generous is:
My love is good and kind.

My love has wit to share;
She's happy after.
Under her clouded hair
We tell our laughter.
The bird sings in the blood
When she is in this mood:
My love has wit to share.

My love has silk and lace
To take delight in;
She lends her clothes such grace
They shine like satin
Nor enviously hide
The girl they have inside:
My love has silk and lace.

My preety love is true;
She'd not deceive me.
The hour I shall know
That she will leave me
For when she tells a lie
It quarrels with her eye:
My preety love is true.

And I would have you so.
I'll always bless you
And let the winds blow—
But I shall miss you:
And please remember this.
The world's a lonely place
And I would not have you so.

IV

Now the winter tree's in leaf,
Crops are ripening for the knife;
Sun and bird and she are kind
But a blade is in the mind

And a wind is in the wood
Stirring fevers in the blood
And the opening of the pear
Fills the knocking heart with fear.

What is it? When she has gone
There is nought to look upon
And her image in the brain
Steals all action from the man.

Let her now return. From sleep
Colours wake, larks leap;
But the subtle knife is keen.
I am quite consumed by pain.

V

He is the season's fool
And nothing earns but banter
Who sighing meets his girl
As if he did not want her.
Oh such a spendthrift of his care
Shall find he'll lie with nought but air.

He is a fool who'd find
In flowering tree a hurt
And let a ghost of wind
Or woman haunt his heart.
Of wind and hair his rope shall be
And he shall blossom on the tree.

He is the fool of Time
Who'd tinker with the minute
Because the mocking worm
Curls like a spring within it.
Before his time the earth he'll wear
And grow green grass instead of hair.

FAR OTHER WORLDS

A white wind turns the daylight moon
And Time is whittled on that stone
Where fat heart sits when he is fed
And whets his grief when he is lean.

The living light upon that ice
Is transient amber in saints' eyes;
There lovers wonder and, love gone,
Grief's torture-pointed comets rise.

There flares the tree the mystics burn
And there is bent the tree of thorn
And griefs dog-buried in that land
Shall stand up green between the stone.

SPEAK WITH THE SUN

From a wreck of tree in the wash of night
Glory, glory, sings the bird;
Across ten thousand years of light
His creative voice is heard.

Wide on a tide of wind are set
Warp and woof of silvered air;
But the song slips through the net
To where the myriad galaxies are.

And to the heartbeats of the light,
Now from the deepness of the glade
Well up the bubbles of delight:
Of such stuff the stars were made.

GLOSSARY OF AUSTRALIAN TERMS

Billycan . .	Tea can.
Blue: Bluey	A tramp's blanket or swag.
Bluey, humping a	Carrying a swag.
Bullocky . .	Teamster.
Burke and Wills .	Explorers: first to cross Australia from south to north; perished on return journey, Burke with a loaded rifle across his chest.
China, over the hills lies	The convicts believed that China lay a short distance beyond the Blue Mountains. Many died in the Bush trying to escape there. The phrase is still current to-day.
Clancy . .	Clancy of the Overflow: shearer and drover ; rides singing through several of Paterson's ballads.
Cocky .	A farmer with a small holding.
Dam . .	Pool.
Darby Munro .	A well-known contemporary jockey.
Dingo . .	Native wild dog.
Hatter . .	A bush madman.

'Hopper swarm .	Plague of grasshoppers.
Jack . .	Laughing Jackass or Kookaburra : a snake-eater; there is a common belief that a scotched snake does not die until after sunset.
Jackeroo . .	Apprentice station or farm manager.
John Bax . .	Coach driver for Cobb & Co.
Kelpie . .	Australian sheepdog, said to be a cross between a Border collie and a fox.
Kid-stakes .	Not fair-dinkum.
Kookaburra .	See " Jack ".
McCoy, the Real	The genuine article.
Shadow of Death, the	A pub at the foot of Conroy's Gap.
Squatter . .	Originally a man who ran his sheep on Crown land; later, any big grazier.
Sundowner . *Swagie* . .	} A tramp.
Swagman, the .	A racehorse celebrated in Banjo Paterson's ballad of *Conroy's Gap*

PRINTED BY
J. W. ARROWSMITH LTD
BRISTOL